Paint and color mixture

Practical steps to achieving the desired color in paint.

Great Nelson

TABLE OF CONTENTS

History

CHAPTER ONE

CHAPTER TWO

CHAPTER THREE

CHAPTER FOUR

Color and Mixing

CHAPTER FIVE

HISTORY

Since prehistoric times, minerals have been utilized as colorants. Paint was employed by early humans for aesthetic purposes such as body ornamentation. Pigments and paint grinding machinery said to be 350,000 to 400,000 years old have been discovered in a cave near Lusaka, Zambia. The first hue of paint was ochre, which was made from iron oxide. Lapis lazuli was used to create a popular blue color. Mineral and clay pigments frequently bear the name of the city or region where they were mined. Raw sienna and burned sienna were sourced in Siena, Italy, while raw umber and burnt umber were sourced in Umbria. These pigments were among the simplest to make, and scientists built contemporary colors on the originals. Colors obtained from the original mineral deposits were more constant, but the location names persisted. Red ochre and hydrated yellow ochre may also be seen in numerous Paleolithic and Neolithic cave paintings. Since prehistoric times, charcoal (or carbon black) has been employed as a black pigment.

Egyptian blue, the first known manufactured color, was discovered on an alabaster bowl in Egypt dated to Naqada III (approximately 3250 BC). Egyptian blue (blue frit), calcium copper, is produced by heating a combination of quartz sand, lime, a flux, and a copper source such as malachite. It was created in Egypt during the Predynastic Period and was widely used by the 4th Dynasty. It was the blue pigment of choice in Roman antiquity, with art technology remains to prove it. vanished in the course of the Middle Ages until its rediscovery in the context of the Egyptian campaign and the excavations in Pompeii and Herculaneum

White lead (basic lead carbonate), vermilion, Verdigris, and lead-tin yellow are examples of later premodern synthetic colors. Vermilion, a mercury sulphide, was initially created by crushing natural cinnabar powder. It was also synthesized from the components beginning in the 17th century. Titian and other great masters appreciated it. Once upon a time, Indian yellow was made by collecting the urine of animals fed exclusively mango leaves.

CHAPTER ONE

<u>COLOR MIXTURE</u>

Color mixing or tinting is one key area producers must be very skilled at. Paints are produced in different colors using colorants that are either in powder form (*known as oxide*) or in paste form (*known as paste*)

Color oxide and paste are both used in secondary color. Red, blue, green, yellow, and black are the primary colors. Most of the paint's hues, so to achieve any color you want to generate other than white/brilliant white, all you have to do is measure the amount that you need in oxide or paste and add to the paint, stirring thoroughly.

Other colors are also available as tertiary hues; in this instance, you must combine three or more colors to get the desired color shade. You must learn how to blend 2-

4 distinct colors to get simply one hue as a

paint   specialist/producer.   The   color

combination recommendations below can

help you differentiate your paint in the

market.

CHAPTER TWO

<u>COLOR RULE</u>

Color rule is the rule such that whenever you are producing paint colors that requires oxide, they are poured inside mixing tank immediately after proper mixing of titanium dioxide but if it is in paste form it come last. This is because paste blend easily with paints than oxide. Oxide required timely and proper mixing to blend with

The color rule, the rule is not whenever you are producing paint colors that required oxide. They are poured inside your mixing tank, immediately after proper mixing of titan, but if it is in paste, it come last. This is because paste blend easily with paints than oxide, oxide required timely and proper mixing to blend with the paint.

What happens if you forget to add color oxide at the beginning or production.

If when producing paint color that require you to add color oxide to your paint formulation at the beginning and you forgot when the paint is ready you must mix the required quantity of color oxide separately in a different container and 1 spoon of Calgon pt and mix the color oxide into a smooth paste, then you add it to the paint and mix for 30 minutes or more.

Below is color and the forms that are available in the market.

COLOR AND FORMS

PASTE - LIQUID

Green paste - liquid paste

Black paste -   liquid paste

Orange paste - liquid paste

Blue paste -   liquid paste

Red paste - liquid paste

Yellow paste – liquid paste

OXIDE – POWDER

Green oxide

Blue chrome oxide

Red oxide

Yellow oxide

Carbon black oxide

Red Scholz oxide

Yellow chrome oxide

Green chrome oxide

CHAPTER THREE

<u>COLOR WHEEL</u>

A color wheel or color circle is an abstract illustrative organization of color hues around a circle, which shows the relationships between primary colors, secondary colors, tertiary colors etc.

When you're learning how to mix paint, keep a color wheel handy to reference. the color wheel takes the full color spectrum and maps it onto a circle. Color theory is founded on the principles outlined in the color wheel, showing the relationships between colors and helping artists to visually see which colors will work harmoniously and which are contrasting. Even expert artists frequently consult their color wheel before embarking on a new project.

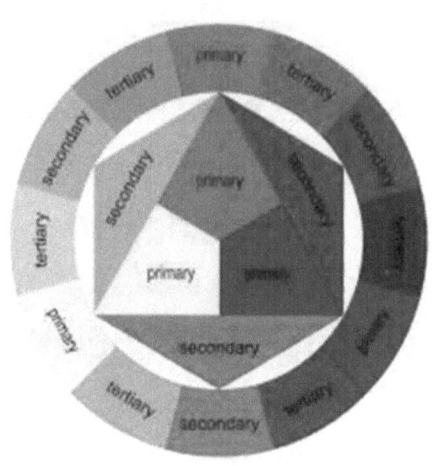

Color wheel

CHAPTER FOUR

<u>COLOR AND MIXING</u>

This color guide serve guideline for your paint color chat and reference, as you produce your paint on a daily basis consult this before you start each production until you are able to get the logic behind formulation and color mixing. The guide is for 30 liters water formulation, that is if you are producing paint with 30 liters of water in your mixing drum, base on the 30 liters measurement or divide if you are producing less than 30 liters of measurement.

Rubine red

Chrome red

Carbon black

Yellow chrome

Chrome oxide

Halogen green

Phthalocyanine

Lemon chrome

Zinc chromate

Brown umber

Prussian

Zinc oxide

Molybdate oxide

Red Scholz

Yellow Scholz

COLORS

Brilliant white - 2-8kg of titanium dioxide, 1-2kg of aluminum silicate.

Off white - 50-100g of yellow oxide after titanium dioxide.

Warm white – titanium dioxide, off white calcium/kaolin or half teaspoon of black paste.

Jasmine white - 2-4 teaspoons of yellow paste.

Blossom white - 2-3 teaspoons of red paste

Almond white - 3-4 teaspoons of yellow paste and 2 teaspoons of red paste.

Basically, white/brilliant white paint color are produced with titan + white calcium carbonate + Aluminum silicate as its color pigments. It does not require any other extra colorants. The combination of titanium dioxide and white calcium + aluminum silicate is the basic requirement to produce basic white or brilliant white. So, if you want the white to be very bright and sharp, you increase the quantity of titanium dioxide + aluminum silicate and ensure you use pure white calcium to produce the paint. For the other whites like off whites, warm whites, jasmine white etc. you do not need pure white calcium and aluminum silicate to produce them, just measure the color as stated in the table and to the paint and mix very well. the above state combo will give you the color shade but it is left for you to increase the deepness of the color or used.

CREAM

Cream 3040 - 250g of yellow oxide after titanium dioxide.

Banana - 100-120g of yellow paste at the end of production.

Canvas - 50-60g of yellow oxide after titanium dioxide.

Bluff -   450g-500g of yellow oxide after titanium dioxide.

Sand - 500g- 1kg of yellow oxide after titanium dioxide and 2 -3 teaspoons of red paste at the end of production

Jasmine - 100g of yellow oxide after titanium dioxide, 50g of yellow paste at the end of production.

Pale beige - 200g of yellow oxide after titanium dioxide, 1-2 teaspoon of black paste.

Pale mushroom - 500g of yellow oxide 2-3 teaspoon of red paste 2-3 teaspoon of black past, depending on the shade desired.

Sun flower - 600g of yellow oxide after titanium dioxide.

Cream colors are basically achieved with yellow oxide for some or in combination with other color pigments for some colors like sand, pale mushroom that requires combination with other colors oxide /pigment to achieve a particular color.

Basic cream colors like cream, off whites, banana, bluff bluff is gotten with just yellow oxide (yellow powder) but in different quantities, for example, 50-100g of yellow in 3 drums of emulsion formulation will give you off white, while 250-300g will give you cream, from 400g-1kg will give you another shade of cream. Its left for you to decide how many quantities you want to use for a particular paint formulation.

Also encourage you to play with different quantities of color oxide/paste and explore other color shade that you can customized

for your paint company.

GREY

Ice grey - 50g of blue paste, 2 spoon of

black paste.

Silver grey - 70g of blue paste, 1 spoon of

black paste.

Gruden – 100g of blue paste, 1 spoon of

paste.

Neutral – 50-70g of yellow paste, 50-60g of black paste at the end of production.

Dove grey – 70g of black paste, 70g of yellow paste.

Dark grey – 150g of black paste, 1 spoon of blue paste at the end of production.

Dusty grey – 100g of yellow oxide, 100g of black paste,50g of yellow paste.

Rock grey – 150g of black paste,100g of yellow oxide.

BLUE

Light blue (SS110) – 2 spoons of blue paste at the end of production

Nursery blue (7084) – 50 grams of blue paste + 2 spoon of yellow paste

Aquamarine (7079) – 50g of blue paste, 4 spoon of yellow paste

Pacific blue (8084) – 100g of blue paste, 50g of yellow paste.

Navy blue – 200g of blue paste, 1 spoon of black paste, 1 spoon of yellow paste.

Sky blue – 4 spoons of blue paste, 1 spoon of yellow paste.

Lagoon blue – 50g of yellow oxide, 1 kg of blue paste.

GREEN

Leaf green (6071) – 200g of yellow paste, 30-40g of blue paste.

Light green (6070) – 100g of yellow paste, 15g of blue paste.

Apple green (6072) - 200g of yellow paste, 30-40g of blue paste, 1 spoon of black paste.

Army green – 100g of yellow oxide, 1kg of green paste, 2 spoon black paste.

Olive green – no titanium dioxide, because it's a deep color 1kg of yellow oxide, 50g of blue paste at the end of production.

National green – 1kg of green paste.

Spray green – 50g of yellow oxide,1 spoon of green paste

Gossamer – 1 teaspoon of chrome yellow, 1 teaspoon of yellow paste, half teaspoon of green paste.

RED

You may also find yourself wondering how to make red paint by mixing colors, but remember, red is a primary color, which means that no other colors can be combined to create it. As you're mixing paint colors, you can combine secondary colors with red to make deeper shades of red like burgundy or lighter colors like pink, but you won't be able to create pure red.

Chinese red – 200g of red oxide, 1 kg of red paste, 1tea spoon of black paste.

Calabash – 10g of yellow oxide, 5g of black paste, 1tea spoon of red paste.

Coral rose – 20g of yellow oxide, 10g of red oxide,1 spoon of red paste.

Brick red – 500g of red oxide, 2 kg of red paste, 1 kg of black paste

Tan SS864- 2 and half teaspoons of red paste (rubine red) at the end of production.

Pale pink SS865 – 5 teaspoons of red paste at the end.

Petal pink SS866 – 5 teaspoons of red paste, 1 teaspoon of yellow paste both at the end of production.

Lilac 1016 - 5 teaspoons of red paste, 1 teaspoon of yellow paste, 1-2 teaspoons of blue paste.

Rose1021 – 100g of red paste, 2 spoon of yellow paste.

Neutral 9094 – 50-60g of yellow paste, 50-60g of black paste.

DEEP COLORS

Tangerine – 150g of yellow paste, 50g of orange paste.

Pale red 0004 – 200g of red oxide at the beginning of production, 1 spoon of blue paste

Coffee SS863 – 1.5 kg yellow oxide, 200g of red oxide, 1 spoon of black paste

Copper SS860 – 1.5 kg of yellow oxide, 200g of red oxide both at the beginning of production

Clinamen 2028 – 200g of red oxide, 3 spoon of blue paste.

Brown – 2kg of red oxide, 300g of yellow oxide, 150g of black paste.

Chocolate – 600g of red oxide, 300g of yellow oxide, 50g of black paste

Post office red – 200g of red oxide, 1kg of red paste.

Rubine red – 1-2kg of red oxide, 250g of red paste

Rich brown - 1.5kg of red oxide, 4 teaspoons of yellow paste

Green gage – Yellow + Blue

Pale beige – Yellow + Red

Pale mushroom – Black + Red + Yellow

Midnight blue - Blue

Bamboo – Red + Yellow

Cameo – Red + Yellow

Sienna – Red + Black + Yellow

Sunflower - Yellow

Tile red – Red

Rose pink – Red

Sand – Yellow + Red

Laterite red - Red + Yellow

Golden yellow – Yellow

CHAPTER FIVE

<u>CONCLUSION</u>

The amount of color you use defines the depth of the color you want. It is also recommended that you write down the exact amount of colorant that you use in each liter of paint that you make. This will aid in the maintenance of balance and homogeneous paint colors. Color alignment, color rule and color wheel are required for the manufacturing of high-quality paint.

The combination of these three will result in a stunning product that you will be proud of.

Color mixing and comprehension of color combination is the most significant component of paint manufacturing that demands enough attention so as not to squander resources that are rare in the market, whether you want to go into paint production or you are currently in the industry. The hue of the paint can be claimed to have influenced paint manufacturing.

www.ingramcontent.com/pod-product-compliance
Lightning Source LLC
Chambersburg PA
CBHW050523290526
45786CB00007B/2670